P9-CMT-498

Maryland

By Susan Labella

Consultants

Reading Adviser
Nanci R. Vargus, EdD
Assistant Professor of Literacy
University of Indianapolis, Indianapolis, Indiana

Subject Adviser
Cheryl Evans
Catonsville Library
Catonsville, Maryland

Children's Press®
A Division of Scholastic Inc.
New York   Toronto   London   Auckland   Sydney
Mexico City   New Delhi   Hong Kong
Danbury, Connecticut

Designer: Herman Adler Design
Photo Researcher: Caroline Anderson
The photo on the cover shows the Baltimore, Maryland, skyline at night.

Library of Congress Cataloging-in-Publication Data

Labella, Susan, 1948–
  Maryland / by Susan Labella.
      p. cm. — (Rookie read-about geography)
  Includes index.
  ISBN 0-516-25256-9 (lib. bdg.)   0-516-25493-6 (pbk.)
  1. Maryland—Juvenile literature. 2. Maryland—Geography—Juvenile
literature. I. Title. II. Series.
  F181.3.L34 2005
  917.52—dc22   2005004031

CHILDREN'S PRESS, and ROOKIE READ-ABOUT®,
and associated logos are trademarks and/or registered trademarks
of Scholastic Library Publishing. SCHOLASTIC and associated logos
are trademarks and/or registered trademarks of Scholastic Inc.

1 2 3 4 5 6 7 8 9 10 R 14 13 12 11 10 09 08 07 06 05

Where is milk the state drink?

In Maryland!

Maryland is on the East
Coast of the United States.

Can you find Maryland
on this map?

5

Farmers in Maryland raise dairy cows. One cow can give about 8 gallons of milk each day!

Maryland farmers also raise chickens.

Some farmers grow crops
such as corn and soybeans.

The largest body of water in Maryland is the Chesapeake Bay. People catch blue crabs in the bay.

Bald eagles make their nests near the bay.

Other birds live in
Maryland, too. The state
bird is the Baltimore oriole.

This is the Druid Hill Park Conservatory.

Maryland has many beautiful gardens. Some are vegetable gardens and others are flower gardens.

The state flower is the black-eyed Susan.

You can see different
kinds of land in Maryland.
In the northwest, there
are mountains with
hiking trails.

Backbone Mountain is
the highest point.

Many people come to
Maryland for its beaches.

They have fun playing in
the sand and swimming
in the Atlantic Ocean.

Some come to see the wild
ponies on Assateague Island.
This island is part of
Maryland's Eastern Shore
and part of Virginia.

The capital of Maryland is
Annapolis. Annapolis has
been called the Sailing
Capital of the World.

Look at this map. Can you
guess why?

SCALE 1 inch = 50 miles

0 Miles 50

0 Kilometers 80

North
West — East
South

23

Annapolis is home to the U.S. Naval Academy. Students go there to become officers in the U.S. Navy or Marines.

The largest city in Maryland is Baltimore. In Baltimore, you can visit an aquarium, a science center, a zoo, and much more!

There are so many places
to visit in Maryland.

Which ones would
you choose?

Words You Know

Assateague Island

bald eagle

Baltimore oriole

beaches

Chesapeake Bay

chickens

crabs

U.S. Naval Academy

31

Index

About the Author

Susan Labella is a freelance writer. She is the author of several books in the Scholastic News nonfiction readers series.

Photo Credits

Photographs ©2005: Alamy Images/Fritz Poelking/Elvele Images: 12, 30 top right; Corbis Images: 28 (David Brooks), 19, 20, 30 bottom right, 30 top left (Kevin Fleming), 27 (Richard T. Nowitz), 24, 31 bottom right (Paul A. Souders); DanitaDelimont.com/Jerry & Marcy Monkman: 9; Folio, Inc./Jim Pickerell: 11, 31 bottom left; Getty Images: cover (Jerry Driendl/Taxi), 15 (Santokh Kochar/Photodisc Green); Index Stock Imagery/Mark Gibson: 14; Photo Researchers, NY/Maslowski: 13, 30 bottom left; PhotoEdit/David Young-Wolff: 3; Ric Ergenbright: 6; The Image Works: 8, 31 top right (David Fraizer), 16 (Jeff Greenberg).

Maps by Bob Italiano